CW00675094

Clasp

First published in 2015 by
The Dedalus Press
13 Moyclare Road
Baldoyle
Dublin 13
Ireland

www.**dedaluspress**.com

ISBN 978 1 910251 02 7

Dedalus Press titles are represented in the UK by
Central Books, 99 Wallis Road, London E9 5LN
and in North America by Syracuse University Press, Inc.,
621 Skytop Road, Suite 110, Syracuse, New York 13244.

Cover image by Natalia Moroz, with thanks.
www.nataliamoroz.com

The Dedalus Press receives financial assistance from
The Arts Council / An Chomhairle Ealaíon

Clasp

Doireann Ní Ghríofa

DEDALUS PRESS
DUBLIN, IRELAND

ACKNOWLEDGEMENTS

I wish to thank the editors of the following journals, in which a number of these poems or versions of them first appeared: *BODY, Cyphers, Numéro Cinq* (Canada), *Poetry Ireland Review, Popshot* (England), *Recours au Poème* (France), *Rose Red Review* (USA), *Southword, The Irish Examiner, The Irish Times, The Pickled Body, The Rotary Dial* (Canada), *Cultural Weekly* (USA). *The SHOp*, and *The Stinging Fly*.

Inventory, Recovery Room was shortlisted for the Strokestown Poetry Prize 2014. *Landslide* was shortlisted for the Mslexia Poetry Prize (UK, 2013). Several of the poems in this collection were also long-listed for the Venture Award (UK, 2013) and others were broadcast on RTÉ Radio 1 and on BBC N.I.

My thanks are due to the Arts Council of Ireland, whose award of a literature bursary in 2013 allowed me to work on this collection. My heartfelt thanks also to Paula Meehan, Ireland Professor of Poetry, for awarding me the Ireland Chair of Poetry bursary, granting me time to finish this collection at the Tyrone Guthrie Centre.

I am very grateful to my co-conspirators in words and ideas: Sara Baume, Leanne O'Sullivan, Cal Doyle, Michelle Callaghan, Rosamund Taylor and filmmaker Peter Madden. Pat Boran at Dedalus Press was exceptionally kind with his time in preparing this book. Thanks too, to Patrick Cotter and Jennifer Matthews at the Munster Literature Centre, whose generosity and encouragement are deeply appreciated.

Contents

꘎

CLASP

harvesting vellum / 11
The Horse Under the Hearth / 12
Rondelet on the Alchemy of Bacon Fat / 13
Valise of Memories / 14
Maeve in Chile / 15
Triolet from the keeper of childhood memories / 16
Instructions To Kill a Daughter's Minotaur / 17
Museum / 19
Frozen Food / 20
After School / 21
In the Post Office / 22
Narcissus / 23
In IKEA / 24
Landslide / 25
Bone Flute / 26
Waking / 27
Holding a Stranger's Hand / 28
The Headless Woman / 29
Lighthouse / 30
I carry your bones in my body / 32
Jigsaw / 33
Inventory: Recovery Room / 34
From Richmond Hill / 35

꘎

CLEAVE

Your Throat, a Thrush / 39
On Bringing a First Child to School / 40
Cocoon / 41
On Patrick Street / 42
Call / 43
Birthburst / 44
Our Mother Who Art Missing / 45
The Light Thief / 46
Tooth / 49
Aubade in a Tumble Dryer / 50
Aftermath: Show Garden / 51
Electrocardiogram / 52
A History in Hearts / 53
Cleaving a Puzzle-Tree / 54
Ascensor / 55
a string, unstrung / 56
tapetum lucidum / 57
How to Steal Trees / 59
Over the Colletine Monastery / 60
We Small Cartographers of Walls / 61
At Letterfrack / 62

~

CLENCH

Seven Views of Cork City / 67

~

Notes / 74

To Tim, without whom
these poems could never have been written:
for Saturday mornings, for endless coffees
and endless kindnesses,
thank you.

Clasp

harvesting vellum

peel away layers of skin
and find again

the hidden digits
once written on this wrist

blue ink on flesh, blue ink
over skin and vein,
blue ink of a number, a name

it's still there, just as under layers
of lip

lies the fossil
of a first kiss.

The Horse Under the Hearth

Quiet now, his stables. No clatter-hoof on the cobbles.
That morning: her saddle bloody, askew, and she
all stumble-legged, froth-flecked, nostril-blaze, trailing reins.
When her eyes found mine, I knew.

I took three leaps: the first over the threshold, the second
to the gate, the third to her back, then fast gallop
over boreen and trampled brambles to his spilled blood.

Everyone knows what happened then, I versed it strong
and spoke it often. But what of her?
Her neck, like mine, knew the rough stubble of his cheek.
I couldn't leave her with them. I sent them out, his men.

And so, her head came back, in a wet sack that leaked in my lap
and reddened my skirts. I pulled the burlap back, looked
into her eyes— sunken, unseeing—
her ear torn, a delicate nostril crushed.

The earth sighed when the hearthstone was pried away.
The fire and I watched as they dug. No one spoke.
I rolled her head into the hole, watched them
shelter her in dirt and stone.

Now, when I watch flames consume wood, I think of her
slow change from muscle and mane to bone and dirt.
When the house grows too quiet, I stand on that hearthstone
and dance. Each ankle tap, each heel rap brings me back

to those fast moments before
we found him, and again, it is only
us two, and we are galloping
and galloping and never reaching him.

Rondelet on the Alchemy of Bacon Fat

I fry rashers
to bring you back. Your laughter burns.
I fry rashers
and taste you on toast, sauce-slathered.
Where hot bacon squirms, you return,
spitting oil. My pan weeps, rinds curl
when I fry rashers.

Valise of Memories

*In memory of Margaret Maher, housemaid & confidante
of Emily Dickinson*

My mistress filled my valise with her vowels —
the battered trunk that journeyed with me
from the shadow of Slievenamon.
Now she is dead.

She made me promise to feed her papers to the flames;
I cannot yet bring myself to do the deed.
I try to dismiss their wild whispers
but they hit their fists against the walls
and stamp their syllables. They long to live
in the mouths and minds of strangers.
All day I fumble, spill soup on my apron,
catch my fingers in the mangle.
The soft grey wool of my mind
is marked by dropped stitches.

Though I keep my chest clasped shut,
I cannot quieten their pleading. Their stifled shrieks
shake me from sleep. I stumble to the chest,
raise the lid, scratch a match.
The flame stares at her scribbled papers.

Pinching the spark, I quench it
and lift the papers from darkness,
one by one.

Maeve in Chile

In Valparaiso, we are drunk again on Pisco sours.
I hunger for food that I cannot name, and
we stumble into a night café, where you feed me
potatoes with lengua. You wait for me
to grimace like the other gringos, but

                                                I smile.

I know the shape of a dead tongue in my mouth,
strong muscle meat, grey, heavy. I cut a chunk.
The root is thicker, tougher than I remember,
and when it slides down my throat, I think of home:
of scrubby grass turned to cud on tongues, of ragwort, of furze.
I think of torn hands stacking stone walls to keep bullocks in
and raiders out. I think of forgotten words that sit in gaps
between grey rocks, between grey clouds, between grey drops.
I think of the frantic low moan of the cow who calls her calf back.
I've never been so far from home. No. I've never been so close.
                    I turn to you and ask for more.

Triolet from the keeper of childhood memories

You must remember that day,
The sun shone, remember? We brought you up to the lake.
We kept trying to warn you, but you being you, you had to
    disobey.
You must remember that day!
It was your sixth …? No, let me think … seventh birthday.
No, no, your costume was blue. Yes, I am sure. For God's sake!
You must remember that day,
the sun shone, remember? We brought you up to the lake.

Instructions To Kill a Daughter's Minotaur

Listen, sister,   it's simple: just do as mother did with us.
Catch her   as she returns from the well. She'll drop
the bucket,   she'll yelp, spill water.
Let the thirsty   sand swallow it.
You'll need two   of you to lift her, clever girl,
she'll know   by now where you are taking her.
Carry her   through the labyrinth of lanes,
to the red   house that sits at its heart. Knock twice.
Close your ears   to her bawling.
Her eyes will be   so white, rolled back
and she will use   all her words to beg you
to release her. Do   not yield, sister.
Hold her. Hold her   down.
Do not let her see   the blade. She'll scream,
better to push a rag to her   mouth —
she will scream. We all   screamed.
Have someone pull her legs   open. You must cut carefully
until you feel the flesh give, the   gush, the shudder,
the heat of torn muscle, the bleeding   meat. When she stills,
you'll know that you've freed her from that   evil root.
Let her weep, but don't lift the rag from   her mouth.
Whisper, don't scare her. Poor child,   poor child,
poor blood of our blood. Press   a clean cloth
to the wound, whisper prayers   to her, sister,
rub her brow smooth, let her blood   clot and cool.
Lift the skein then, the spool of red   thread.
You may weaken, but remember,   it is you
who hold the ball of thread   and you who must help her
to find her way away from   this place.
Run your needle through   the candle flame, sister.
Each stitch is a step back   home.

17

You must bring her back,   sister,
— so stitch her neat — stitch   her tight.
Knot the thread, put the skein   on the shelf for the next.
Now you can smile, sister,   and sing the old lullabies
that soothed her   when she screamed
eight summers   ago, your little calf, your screechling,
your womb-raw   daughter. You birthed her once, sister.
Now you must   birth her again,
        from   blood.

— · — · —

Museum

I am custodian of this exhibition of erasures, curator of loss.
I watch over pages of scribbles, deletions, obliterations,
in a museum that preserves not what is left, but what is lost.

Where arteries are unblocked, I keep the missing clots.
I collect all the lasered tattoos that let skin start again.
In this exhibition of erasures, I am curator of loss.

See the unravelled wool that was once a soldier's socks,
shredded documents, untied shoestring
knots — my museum protects not what is left, but what is lost.

I keep deleted jpegs of strangers with eyes crossed,
and the circle of pale skin where you removed your wedding
        ring.
I recall all the names you ever forgot. I am curator of loss.

Here, the forgotten need for the flint and steel of a tinderbox,
and there, a barber's pile of scissored hair. I attend
not what is left, but what is lost.

I keep shrapnel pulled from wounds where children were shot,
confession sins, abortions, wildflowers lost in cement.
I am custodian of erasures. I am curator of loss
in this museum that protects not what is left, but what is lost.

Frozen Food

In the frozen foods aisle, I think of him
when I shiver among shelves of green flecked
garlic breads and chunks of frozen fish.
I touch the cold door until my thumbs numb.

Strangers unpacked his body in a lab
and thawed his hand, watched long-frozen fingers
unfurl one by one, until his fist finally opened,
let go, and from his grasp rolled
a single sloe,
ice-black with a purple-blue waxy bloom.

Inside the sloe,
a blackthorn stone.
Inside the stone,
a seed.

Standing in the supermarket aisle,
I watch my breath freeze.

After School

From across the classroom, on a wave of others' palms,
he sends me scribbled notes.
He waits in the graffiti corner behind the school.
I walk towards him, my skirt rolled up over bare knees.
On his tongue, I taste smoke and chewing gum.
We throw schoolbags aside, bags full of homework
unbegun —
page after empty page to be filled
with irregular verbs of the future tense.

In the Post Office

You press your tongue to a stamp.
Looking up, you catch me watching,
but I can't look away.
You hold my gaze as you lick
and press the stamp to paper.
  Damp.
I want to feel you press against me,
tongue and thumbs
sticking to my skin.

Narcissus

Narcissus tires of talking, snatches his coat and leaves
the thudding nightclub. He shoulders through the shouldering
crowd, sparks a cigarette, strides through a forest of neon
signs, throbbing pubs, stumbling drunks, bouncers, strip-clubs.

Tripping over the threshold of his flat, he
flicks a switch, ignores the prod of his beer-blown bladder,
and pulls a stool to his screen's dark pool.
It brightens with his digital twin,

and Narcissus dabbles fingers through his reflections —
a cascade of windows rippling past, his own image cast back
again and again. He swipes, smiles: so many *likes*, so many
friends. His soundless words flash onto strangers' screens

until silence no longer feels like loneliness.
Narcissus gazes through glass until his eyes ache.
He seeks the comfort of sex-sites, eyes over skin
until he gasps at his own reflected orgasm.

Narcissus tires. Still nothing new in his inbox,
though he keeps a finger idly dabbling,
refresh, refresh, refresh. His head tilts into his palm,
eyes still on the screen until it darkens to standby.

In IKEA

Here, doors lead nowhere. Daisy-print curtains open to concrete.
No spiders build webs, no dust falls. From a forest of frames,
the same strangers grin; soon they feel as familiar as cousins.
We find their belongings strewn around each fake room.
My feet are tired. I start to imagine myself as one of those
framed strangers — cardboard. We wander the floors,
bored burglars, lifting things and putting them back again.

My breath is hot. Come closer, let me whisper:
In my pocket I've hidden an assembly key. It will fit
every flimsy flat-pack here. It unlocks every slot.
I could dismantle all these doors and beds and floors.
We could watch it all fall.

You know, I could take you to pieces too.
I could slip this key between your collarbones,
your earlobes, your thighs. I could unlock all your sockets.
Come behind this cupboard. Open your buttons.
Let me unpack you.

Landslide

We were there that day, in Thistle, Utah
the day wet clay began to bury the city.

From the attic window, we saw all the others
hustled away on buses. The swamp rose,

slow at first, trickle to stream to gush. When we
held hands, the lines on our palms sparked.

Mud dammed the creeks, sent surges of dirt-water
to swallow the sidewalks. It heaved houses aside,

toppled poles, smothered cars, snapped doors.
We stared until everything blurred.

Train tracks buckled in its path.
Railcar roofs became rafts, their carriages sank.

Mud settled to silt on the roads and in our throats.
Our memories faded, buried in the filth,

so we started our stories again. We learned
new words and spoke in syllables of murk.

Now, when night sinks,
we swallow each other like silk.

Bone Flute

Far above, they watch your wings beat — slender, white.
A stone knocks you, stops your return to the nest.
Their hunger is sharp, it jerks you from the sky;
in death, you are gathered to a stranger's chest.

Inside, they tell your story with hands and grunts.
So fast, you go from flight to fire — your plumage plucked,
beak broken, feet cut —
so fast, you become a chunk of meat to be cooked.

A girl finds your wing bone, whittles it to a whistle,
punctures it with holes. She lifts it to her lips and blows,
making of you something more than meat and gristle.
From mute remains, music rises among crows.

Breath into bone, her air raises you. She lifts your wing
and, over dark hills, a new sound sings.

Waking

for Savita Halappanavar

The procedure complete, I wake alone.
The hospital sleeps. My fingers fumble
over a new scar, jagged map
stitched into my skin —
empty without and empty within.
I trace the wound and weep.

The only sound I hear now
is the retreat of a doctor's footsteps,
echoing my heartbeat.

Holding a Stranger's Hand

You were there too, were you? Do you remember the foxgloves?
All along our avenue, those purple bells filled with pollen and
    pale freckles
nodded at us as we strolled home from a dance, at dusk.

You must be... Yes, you are. Who are you again, love?
Yes, I knew that. It was ... *Méiríní sí,* Mother said — fairy
    thimbles,
and butterflies and bumblebees. Do you remember? The foxglove

blossoms were everywhere — tall, leafy, lush —
and nodding, always nodding. Birdsong and bicycle bells
lit the air when we strolled home from the dance. At dusk,

the foxgloves were plump, soft pops between fingers and thumbs.
The bushes burst with them, the hedges all purple-speckled.
You were there, weren't you? You remember the foxgloves,

their lips pursed, like a sigh stifled, like a mother's blush.
The sun sank slow, painted our faces gold as honeysuckle.
You remind me of someone who strolled home with us.

Around the eyes, maybe ... What's your name again, love?
Why are you crying? Don't lie, I can feel your hands tremble.
Ah, I see. You're remembering the shivering foxgloves
and my hand in yours, the night we strolled home from a dance,
    at dusk.

The Headless Woman

The locket lost, we keep the snapshot:
you in sunlight, leaning on a bonnet,
ankles crossed, in a summer dress.
A jagged white gap sits on your shoulders.

Somewhere, a stranger thumbs
the broken clasp of a metal heart
to see your bodiless face
smiling against sunlight,
and remembers a you we never knew.

Lighthouse

My childhood is a lighthouse in a slate-grey sea.
Every night, I look back. Sometimes, I think I see the light.
My eye searches until it aches, but all that is, is dark.
I stare into the night over a thousand black waves,
but the horizon remains, unbroken.
I sit at my window, willing the flash to come again.

In my dreams, I skip again
in a house I know by heart. It stands white against a gruff sea.
The Tilley lamp holds my hand as I crunch over broken
bulbs to the rusted clockwork cogs that turn in the guts,
        sending light
to protect ships from rocks and drunken waves.
In dreams, I'm unafraid. On my own, it's easy to be brave.
        Even in the dark.

It's with people that trouble starts. My mind runs up the stairs,
        past dark
bedrooms, past the boiler that ticks like a hollow heart. Higher
        again
I run, to the lantern room. Breathless, I watch waves,
clenched fists breaking into sea,
spitting curses. I stand by the bulb, feel the light's
heat on my back. I cast my shadow out into the night, a broken

reflection. Below, the sea churns, green as shards of broken
glass. Is it sea? Or is it my city? I rub my eyes. Traffic rocks
        like froth on dark
rain roads. Double-deckers sail by. From pubs, seasick men
        stagger against streetlights.
This is my lighthouse, this is where I grew up— the Flats. Again,

I stand in the tallest tower, squint over an ocean of concrete,
  to see
my stepfather. He always stops on his way back, puts down his
  bag of cans and waves,

waves up at me with wild-arms, laughs and waves and waves.
This is my tower of cracked things: jammed lifts, arrowed
  hearts, broken
teeth. In the basement, the boiler bangs, dark heart. See,
it was here that I grew up with brown pebbles in tracksuit
  pockets, dark
tattoos of pin and Indian ink, pizzas in plastic again.
Home. Our tower beamed into city nights. This was my house
  of a thousand lights.

When I heard they tore it down, I grew to miss that old lighthouse. I left my childhood there, behind a wall of waves.
Its shadow sent me strength to stand, even when hit again and
  again.
It broke others. It even broke itself, in the end. I couldn't be
  broken.
I chose to live on land, but my horizon is too empty now, too
  dark.
Sometimes I think I feel it behind me. I imagine that I see

it in the dark. I loved that lighthouse — it made me. A broken
home is still a home, where waves of traffic sing a lullaby
  through dark.
I will build a new lighthouse and put a child there, high above
  the wild sea.

I carry your bones in my body

I carry you in my body
little skeleton
little skull
— nobody — nearlybody — my small someone.

I carry you in my body
little skeleton
little skull
somebody — nobody — a tangled knot, undone.

Jigsaw

For months, all I knew of you
was a jumble of limbs, a muddle of joints
moving like shadows under my skin—
the prod of knee or elbow,
the roll of foot or hip.

When you slid from me   to me
I spent hours piecing your jigsaw
together in slow recognition—
how the arch of your foot
fit the hollow of my palm,
how your head nestled
into the curve of my neck.

We fit, you and I—
familiar stranger,
unknown made known.

Inventory: Recovery Room

A thin yellow curtain shivers around my bed.
The IV stand bows its metal head
and a clipboard displays falling numbers.

On the windowsill, empty-eyed bottles stare at rain.
A plastic plug lies on the tile, severing TV from socket.
The screen is black now and shows only my reflection:

pale face, blue gown, surgical socks stretched up to the crotch.
My breasts are funnelled into plastic cups. The machine
whine-whirrs, stretches my flesh, lets go again;

the feeling as strange as a pinned and needled leg.
Still, nothing happens
until I think of milk, of beestings squeezed from a cow's udders,

of my fingers between a calf's gums: the fierce suck of a new
          mouth,
and the echo of a mother's angry bellows from the field.
Within my chest, an itch begins to stir. The machine's slow suck

and release yields a single drop of yellow liquid.
A second slow drop forms and falls ... Another.
Another. I sit and feed the machine, politely, quietly.

Electricity pulls milk from me as I continue my inventory —
by the wall, an empty cot, a hand-knit blanket,
a small white hat and an unused nappy, flat.

From Richmond Hill

Home from hospital, you doze in my arm, milk-drunk,
all eyelashes, cheeks and raw umbilical, swaddled
in the heavy black smells of the brewery.

Your great-grandfathers worked all their lives in that factory.
Every day they were there, breathing the same air, hoisting
barrels, sweating over vats where black bubbles rose like fat.

At dusk, they poured into pubs, and ordered porter,
neat black pints lidded with white silk, thick as cream
from frothing milk, and their replies were always the same:

the gasp, the nod. Down gullets and guts went the porter,
went the pay, went the nights and days. Every day
the same — coins slapped on the counter. No change.

In my arms, you stir. A thousand streetlamps
flicker to light in the dusk. As I watch your eyes open,
the reek of roasting hops knits a blanket of scent around us.

Cleave

Your Throat, a Thrush

At red, the car stops.
My thumbs drum on the steering wheel.
On top of the traffic light, a bird is perched,
speckled belly-feathers ruffled, beak split open
by song. I think of his throat, of the syrinx
nestled where the windpipe splits,
the organ that gives him two voices, two songs.

A twin whistling turns my mirror-glance back
to you, small son, where suddenly you too,
have the throat of a thrush. Air spills
from your lungs into sound, a whistling
that tilts clear as sunlight. To look
back at you is to glimpse the past —

and I am with my grandfather again,
car windows wound down,
the backseat sticky with old sunlight.
In the rear-view mirror, his eyes joke with mine.
When he winks, a whistle springs from his smile.

Now, I see him again. He lives in your throat, son,
in your eye as you squint against the sun's glint.
Countless layers fold between our time and theirs
and still, in each new skin, we sing.

The light turns
and the thrush falls up
on dark wings.

On Bringing a First Child to School

On laundry lines I find
a spider on a red peg, and, inside,
a clotted web pressed into the cleft,
grey knot tangled with eggs.

Days later,
filaments of spider-silk spill from line
to path; on each gossamer thread,
spiderlings
bound
to new webs.

Cocoon

Seeing light leak from the crack under his bedroom door,
I hold my breath and tiptoe over the threshold.

Through the day's debris, my feet search for floor,
between piles of plastic dinosaurs, comics, tilting Lego towers.

A light shines from elsewhere — *there* —
the tented sheet. Underneath, a torch glows.

I stand outside.   Apart.

The dark makes a mirror of his window tonight.
I see my reflection there — brown moth, drawn to his light.

On Patrick Street

This part of the path was once a place apart, a tall glass box
with a door that creaked in like pleats of an accordion.

Not long ago, we stood here, where a cord looped long
and pressed a heavy black handset between shoulder and neck.

Here, we fumbled through coins, shoved them
clunk by clunk into a slot, pressed digits

until we heard our need chime in some distant room.
Then, the lift, the click, the answer of the voice we waited for.

There were times, walking past, you might see someone
through glass, rubbing their brow, or laughing, head thrown back,

until knuckles rasped on the door. At dusk it glowed, lit
from within. We don't speak about how it left or where it went.

We hurry past that place on the footpath now, small square
of empty cement, with plastic pressed to our ears, repeating:

Where are you?
I'm here.

Call

No slender thread,
                    no telephone cord
binds us anymore.
Now that our computers call each other,
        I can't
                press your voice to my ear.
No longer can I hear you breathe. Now, we are bound only
                by a weak connection
and we break up
                and break up
        and break up.

Birthburst

many months, to float in warmth
womb-wet swell
stirred with her world-murmur

until
the surges
stir

Now   the caesarean slice
       Now   mother's girl-cries
            Now   the hospital light

through this first rift, flesh-crevice
the lift, the light, the clench and pinch
the cord clamped, cut, the cold, and now,
now the swaddle,
now,

now the stench, as they scorch and stitch her flesh,
fusing this fissure together again:
my path back, sealed tight
so now I must become
I,
I am,
I.

Our Mother Who Art Missing

And then quietly, she disappeared again. With strange smiles in
    our eyes,
we searched and searched for her between the washing lines,
all the slap and flap of her skirts and all the empty spaces between.
She wasn't there. We peered into the dark cave under the stairs,
then searched and searched for her between the washing lines
again. The oven, empty. In the wardrobe, blouses shrugged. Still,
she wasn't there. We peered into the dark cave under the stairs,
where her hats and shoes and coats were all empty. We waited.
Again, the oven. Empty. In the wardrobe, blouses shrugged, still.
We listened to the telephone's dull drone and stared out windows.
    Still no sign
where her hats and shoes and coats were. All empty, we waited.
The cupboards were bare. Still, we searched and searched.
We listened to the telephone's dull drone. We stared out windows,
    still no sign
at all of the slapping flap of her skirts. All the empty spaces between
the cupboards were bare, still. We searched and searched
and then, quietly, she appeared again, a stranger's smile in her eyes.

The Light Thief

1.

In Winter, Mother suffers. She can't report me missing
anymore — the police shrug at her abduction stories.
They know where I go — to the last stop on the underground,

to his windowless basement squat, the stench of piss
and chicken bones in a grease-stained KFC boxes
where we shiver in our sleep on a sheetless mattress.

Mother must have known that I'd bring only
badness to her life. Why else would she name me Perspehone —
she who steals light ?

When I leave, she tears through barren streets like a gale,
fixing posters of me to fences, lamp-posts and trees,
Sellotape spools flashing like gold bracelets on her wrists.

All over the city she glues my grin:
MISSING: PERSEPHONE
Until the posters age and my face fades

under a yellowed skin of tape. One by one,
the letters blur until all that is left is
MISS_____ PERSEPHONE

Mother reads the signs, falls to her knees and weeps.
Winter frosts in her face, silvers her lined brow. Her eyes ice.
The posters taunt her, text and photo weather-erased,

until all that's left is my pale smile, and below:
___IS_____

Those faded posters are right, I exist.
The night is lighter than light to me now.
I hunger for him and what he brings —

the flaming lighter, the scorched pipe,
the path of blackened glass that leads down,
down.

There was no pomegranate, no alchemy of seeds,
just these crystals, crushed, just this smoke
spinning up, just this rush, just this, just us.

2.

Months burn. I weaken, open the narrow door
and walk up steps to light. When I return,
Mother seems much older. She means well, I suppose,

hugging me until her nails leave white moons in my skin,
locking me in again to spend days sitting in circles,
nodding at strangers in the hospital-stench of disinfectant.

I force myself to smile at her during visiting hours,
to tolerate her fingers in my hair, her whispers of
university, her incessant printing of CVs.

I watch April sun touch her skin and try not to think
of him, but I soon weary of her ultimatums,
of bolted doors. I start to dream of him.

I run away again. One by one, he quenches my lights,
blackens veins and arteries, scalds my alveoli.
I lie with him and it is sweet relief to be back below,

back home. Somewhere, Mother
tapes my old face to poles,
her hands colder than cold.

Tooth

You know how it happens: the first wince,
the lingering sting. It sharpens, deepens
until the pain won't let you sleep and you find yourself
in a waiting room, fingernails pinched into slick palms.

A chair tilts you back. Mouth ajar, you hear the latex gloves
— snap snap — and see the syringe. You hold your breath
as anaesthetic heats the flesh of your cheek.
A metal clamp is thrust between your teeth
and the tugging begins, until something in you relents.
The bloodied tooth is tugged from bone, torn clear
from the jaw it was born in. Blood spurts into stuffed gauze.
The dentist lifts the tooth, asks if you want to keep it.
You shake your head: *No*. No — you'll keep
                                        the empty socket, the hole.

Later, what seems strangest is how your tongue,
still numb, slips in and out of the gap,
as it did when you lost your first child-tooth.
This time, though, there will be no patted head, no fairy,
no new tooth. Absence festers in you like an abscess —
the un-held hand, the un-patted back. This time, you are left
with a pocketful of feeble painkillers and cold rain that rolls
under your collar as you wait for the bus home.
Is this what it is to be an adult? Yes. You are alone.

Aubade in a Tumble Dryer

We wake rumpled and thirsty behind a glass eye
after hours of drunken stumbling, whirling
to tunes spun by an unseen DJ,

all elbows and grins and *Tequila! Tequila!*,
our words slurring, falling into each other,
falling and flying, flying and falling, faster, faster …

Now, the rave is over. Dawn-light leaks in: hard, bright.
We wake tangled up in old lovers,
damp arms around each other, suddenly shy,

finding ourselves creased into each other's curves,
our collars crumpled, our sleeves lined.
We avoid each other's eyes

and wait for morning to open the door,
to peel us apart in a jolt of static sparks,
to be ironed and tucked away, apart again.

Aftermath: Show Garden

The cameras and smiling hosts are gone; the makeover is over.
Wood whispers. Nature will wolf us now — it starts to sink in:
the decking disintegrates underfoot, slug and snail
slime stains everything. The bench is slowly splintering,
the wood whispering — *Nature will wolf us. Now, it starts to
    sink in.*
The garden heating system topples and rusts.
Slime stains everything. The bench is slowly splintering
under us. Rats run from the compost corner. A stench of
    rotting vegetables rises
where the garden heating system topples. Rust
infects the steel sculpture of Buddha laughing near the
    meditation pond.
Under us, rats run. From the compost corner, a stench of
    rotting vegetables rises.
Nails weep rust. All the varnished gloss has been lost. Mould
infects the steel sculptures. Buddha laughs at the meditation
    pond.
The decking disintegrates. Under foot, slugs and snails.
Nails weep rust. All the varnished gloss has been lost to mould.
The cameras and smiling hosts are gone. The makeover is over.

Electrocardiogram

Here, a machine listen to bodies.
In heartbeats, it hears
the messages
of valves and vessels,
deciphers
their cyphers,
decodes words and wires them
along coiled cables
to where a needle scrapes on paper
in jagged scrawl.
A scroll unfurls
as the heart scratches
its dispatches of despair
— muscle translated into ink,
a telegram
from within.

A History in Hearts

I sleep.
I sleep and, as I sleep, a surgeon arrives.
He breaks my breastbone,
makes his incisions, suctions liquid,
lifts my heart out,
sets it aside.

Stitch by stitch, he attaches
the heart of a stranger to the stump
and sets it moving like electricity.
Under his hands, a new heart stutters and starts,
filling the cavity with applause. He closes my ribcage.
The machines sing. Inner doors unlock, valves open,
and all my small intricacies nod, whispering:
     come in,   *come in.*
I begin again, by the lift and lull of a stranger's pulse.

Somewhere, in a bag labelled *Medical Waste,*
my old atria turn grey. I dream of soft
ash and wake, and wake, my hands trembling.

Cleaving a Puzzle-Tree

1.

I didn't see my grandmother's tree in Chile,
araucaria araucana,
though they grow tall there and are many.
I must have walked under them every day, tripped
over their seeds, but I didn't think of her, oceans away,
standing in a square of green, raking leaves
around her monkey puzzle tree.

2.

For over a hundred years, that tree stood between
pruned rosebush and clipped hedge, a long shadow
moving over wet fields and stone walls.
As a girl, I clung to the trunk when we played hide and seek,
rough bark printing maps on my palms.

3.

In April gales, the tree sways. From the window,
my grandmother watches a chainsaw blade
spin the tree into a flight of splinters,
until only logs and sawdust are left.
In each neat wheel of wood, an eye opens,
ringed by lines of the past. The logs are split,
stacked, the tree turned into armfuls of firewood
which will rise as smoke to the sky,
a puzzle unravelled.

Ascensor

A funicular, this heart of mine — little more
than a clapboard cabinet on a cord,
drawn by string and whim. Like its sisters,
it see-saws up and down the slopes of Valparaiso.
In this city of cobbled alleys and painted streets,
it grinds a path from ocean to hilltop houses.
Inside, graffiti marks the small, scarred room
where teenagers with penknives once gouged
LOVE. The narrow door opens
and lets more passengers in — children, grandchildren.
The rope that bears such weight grows weak with age,
but every day, it lifts people up the hills and down again.

a string, unstrung

each pearl   a fist   closing on the ocean floor
each pearl   a knuckle bone, white under the weight of vast blue
each pearl   an alveolus   a spasm   in throbbing lungs
each pearl   a breath   blown into water   moving skyward
each pearl   a bubble   air globule   in ocean churn
each pearl   a grain of rice   in the sticky fist of a son,
each pearl   unstrung
each pearl   a song,   unsung

tapetum lucidum

(lines to a distant granddaughter)

wet squelch,
toes numb in boots
that your father put holes in, decades
before   before

before nights of following
a spark through dark,
where torchlight makes
a yellow path in long wet grass,
a blank slant over bog, through
scrape of furze thorn and muddy gaps,
a scramble over loose stone walls
that shudder and shift underfoot
until
two small mirrors shine back from the dark,
a stewable morsel in a soft brown pelt
stands and stares back
and you are

— a hare —

frozen,	frozen,
two faces	in stasis
eyes wild	blazing
bound by	a beam
in a world	of dark
eye to eye	still

[pause.
sing of hunger, sing of night
sing of future, sing of fire
sing of scorched meat
wedged between your teeth]

                                        still, listen:
                                          behind,
            the cold whines of dogs   rise
                  a man curses
        loosens the urge of lurchers into the black

and your lamp
falls.

How to Steal Trees

We recommend night-time robberies.
Wait in the dark until night grows black.
Brush away all leaves.
Empty the sack, ready the tools.
Circle the area with the blade of a spade.
Dig gently to loosen the roots, then sink
your tools deep into the dirt.
Push underneath, holding the root-balls tight.
Lift. Tuck the base into a bag of coarse hessian.
Do not displace the earth. Tie twice with twine.
Worry over damage is needless; young trees are resilient.
Wrap them in in burlap sacks. Fill a van. Don't turn back.
Replant. Grow to required size. Sharpen an axe.

Over the Colletine Monastery

Soft footfall is the only sound
to rustle this convent's silence,
where all day, veiled women
move to bells, until a final chime
sends them to bed. Then,
from gaps under rafters, pipistrelles stir,
ravenous bats scatter to gorge themselves
on midges and moths at the Lough.
Like black blots spilled
between quill and inkwell,
they smudge our nights.
Over the sleeping convent, they follow
sky-paths, stammering through dark,
until light tucks them back under rafters
and, below, bells begin a new day.

We Small Cartographers of Walls

Every day we walked the cracked path to school,
held Mother's hand, hefted our patched satchels.
We knew the route by heart, by touch too,
where our fingers dawdled on bin lids and windowsills.

One wall was darker, taller than the others,
the old stone damp, clammy under our hands —
moss-dappled bricks gripped in crumbling mortar,
and the wall so tall that no one could glance

over. At the steel-railed gate, our feet slowed us
to stare. We knew that others lived their lives inside
but our whispered questions were always shushed.
Behind tall walls and locked gates, secrets hide.

When we asked why, her step quickened.
Mother said: *Some things must be kept hidden.*

At Letterfrack

From the Ryan Report on Industrial School Abuse, Volume 1, Chapter 8, paragraph 162: *"The children would run away at night but they would usually be apprehended, sometimes by local people, and returned to the school soon after."*

I
This bog of flattened bracken was once a vast forest,
filled with wildcats and wolves.
The bog still dreams of trees, buried deep, unseen.

II
Centuries ago, people built togher roads here —
slats of wide wood hauled up and laid side by side
so treacherous wetlands of bog could be crossed.
These roads remain, far below the surface,
where years of peat grow over the past like scabs.
The bog swallows people and their paths.
The bog swallows itself.

III
Later, few trees grow
so people hunt the wood that lies below,
trunks of sunken forests buried in the bog.
At dawn, they seek patches of peat
where dew has disappeared, then pierce
the surface and push long rods deep,
deeper, through gulping ground
until they strike solid wood.
They pull chunks up and make rafters,
doorways, window frames.
From this land, a school and a spire rose.

IV

Behind the school, a path ends at a small gate—
small plot, small stones, where small letters spell small names.
Leaves whisper: there is nothing here to fear.
The earth holds small skulls like seeds.

V

Winter.
Ice grows on dormitory windows. Inside, rows of snores.
Together, two boys whisper and dress in the dark. Hand in hand,
they run through white fields towards home.
Does the land betray them?
No, a wizened hawthorn holds out hands to try to hide them.

VI

In winter, runaways are easily found. Even in the dark,
small bootprints break through white to the ground below.
Does the land betray them?
Yes, it shows their path through snow.

VII

They do not cry as they are dragged back, stripped of clothes,
pushed against the school wall, their small feet sinking into snow.
There, they are beaten and sprayed with a hose.
Does the land protect them?
Yes, it holds their hands in the dark.

VIII

In dormitories of sleeping boys, they shiver and bleed
and weep black bogwater tears. Overhead, rafters dream
of their sunken mothers, submerged still, deep in the bog.
Does the land protect them?
Yes, it stays under their fingernails forever.

IX

By March, the snow has returned to air, the footprints
disappeared. From the earth, buds open white petals to light
where wood anemones fill bog-paths with stars.
Do they hold onto this land?
No, they forget. They let go.

X

The boys grow up. They walk away.
They leave Letterfrack, and go to London, Dublin, Boston.
Through their dreams, the mountain cuts a stark shadow.

Do they hold onto this land?
Yes, it holds them hard always — as a scar silvers from a red welt,
it tightens at the throat like the notch of a belt.

Clench

Seven Views of Cork City

I

No one knows that I wake in the night and creep down
— tiptoe toetip — to watch Granddad's little dog sleep.
I glug milk from the bottle, take a Ginger Nut from the tin
and stand over him. A knot of short fur, snout, soft ears,
he tears through sleep on rough paw-pads. I hear
his sleep-squeaks. Even with eyelids closed, he's chasing
rabbits and rats. His whole body squirms and turns
in a world I'll never see. I wish I could live in a terrier's dream.

I wipe up the crumbs, sneak upstairs to my still-warm bed.
From between the curtains, I read the city like a map.
On the hill, rooftops lean into each other, each
holding warm embers dozing in grates, stacked anoraks,
dark fridges full of food and fireside rugs where other terriers
run through dreams. I am the only one awake —
in this sleeping city, all is silent.

II

All is silent. The car park is empty when we break in,
cold, a hollow tower of echoes where night winds spin,
whistling through each level. An inner road
spirals at its core, concrete through concrete,
floor into floor, round and round
until it reaches the roof.
Here, vacant slots dream of cars. Puddles stare at clouds.
We rattle our cans, tag grey turrets, share a cigarette.
Like the black river below, we'll never be caught.

We are the only people in the city tonight —
our kingdom, a thousand crooked rooftops.

III

our kingdom is a thousand crooked rooftops
these years we spend tripping down
Barrack Street, Grand Parade,
with strangers who become sisters and brothers,
tell them our secrets, our lies, turn ourselves inside out
we make ourselves new and it is a difficult birthing

at night, we do ourselves up by blotched mirrors
with cheap mascara and cheaper wine
false blushes bloom on our cheeks,
fag-butts fizz into cans of cider

every night, we tumble into pubs, squealing over each other,
long lost sisters with shots of Jäger and hands in the air,
strobes, pills under tongues and coke in the jacks,
screeching over beats: best night, best night *ever,*
best friend, *best friends ever* never forget this night, *never*
           Never

but too soon the lights are back and we're barefoot, staggering,
carrying each other home, the sky spins and we sing and sing,
someone is puking on a doorstep, and we are holding handfuls
of hair and whispering you'll be OK, OK, OK …
our thirst subsides suddenly, displaced by an ancient hunger
and so, we always end our nights with the same ritual:
staring up at bright menus, thinking only of chips,
chips, chips, and we're sitting barefoot on the path outside
           Lennox's,
heels cast aside, potato steam rising from folded paper

like a long-forgotten prayer and our mouths all holy Os of awe,
and we're watching our hot breath
float
into the city night and wondering where it will go
and wondering where we will go

IV

Where will we go? Where could we go? Nowhere.
Confined to neat rows of narrow beds, we wait.
In the college morgue, stained sheets
are pulled up over every head,
falling in folds over our thin legs,
cold stomachs, flaps of bloodless skin.
Orange streetlights peer at us through bare windows.
Our eyes don't see now. If we could see, all would be white.
The students are all gone — drinking, laughing, sleeping.
When they lift morning scalpels to our skin, we hear
the dull thump of a pulse in wrists close to our ears.
We smell their breath, their hangovers.
We lie in the dark and wait for something to start.
We wait. Our tired minds settle into silence.

V

My tired mind settles into silence as disinfectant evaporates
from my hands. The small screen lights up. 'Where are you?'
I type: 'In the Mercy' my finger hovers over SEND
then letter by letter — delete — delete —
I stare at the blank screen until it goes black.

Below: an ambulance, door thrown open,
people running,
a sheet tucked tight over a stretcher,

a mouth hangs open,
blood under blue lights. And then gone.

The light above me hums, fluorescent cylinders flickering.
I look over the dark river, swollen, surging in from Sunday's
Well,
brimming with the liquid weight of the west. Behind me,
footsteps come and go along the corridor.
A student doctor approaches, flicking the tip of her pen, again,
again. She nods as she strides by.
I try not to think of you. I look at the water and remember

that sunny afternoon at Gougane Barra,
the squashed sandwiches,
our hop over the slender stream that starts the Lee,
your fingers in mine for the first time,
a tingle
like the static shock of tumble-dried clothes.

You know, I would rewind the river to take us back there,
unrun the current,
unfork the island streams,
reverse through the sluice,
return over the weirs,
through Carrigrohane, Macroom, Inchigeelagh, Ballingeary,
up to the forest at Gougane.
I would climb the hill,
wind the stream back into the ground.
We would jump over it,
backwards this time, hand in hand.

How did we jump from there to here? Too fast.
Footsteps again.
A grey doctor in scrubs walks past.

The corridor quietens.
I wait for news.
I watch the lights go out one by one in distant bedrooms,
imagining all the sleep, all the warmth,
all those duvets and dreams. I wait, and watch
sleepless seagulls slip over the river,
over Cork's hills, over cathedrals and car-parks.

VI

Over Cork's hills, over cathedrals and car-parks,
that bat flew and made its way to me in Tesco.
Started as usual, clocked in at ten, nightshift till six,
sweeping, wiping, stacking shelves. I walked up
and down aisles with my broad bristled brush
past tired midwives in blood-spattered scrubs, then out
to the dark car park to gather stray trollies
and slot them into each other, steel in steel,
tucked in neatly to dream of speed.
The maternity hospital stared down at me,
a new life bursting out behind each lit window.
Inside again, a head-phoned boy-racer struts up to me,
two tins of baby formula and a titty mag under an elbow,
grunts "Where's the beer?" I point my broom-handle
to Aisle 15, and walk upstairs to the store room.
I must have looked up just then, and saw it there,
saw the bat, so sudden, so fast, and just like *that*,
I swung the brush up.
Reflexes, like. The bat fell at my feet.
I lifted it. Warm. Furry. Its face was ... peaceful, soft,
like a baby's. It had tiny dead eyes.
I stopped on the third step and felt my whole being, all of me
clench.

I stop on the third step and feel my whole being, all of me
                    clench
          release
      breathe deep.
Christ. I walk the corridors again, walk and wait.
It's good, walking, it gets me away from the ward
and all those nosy nurses and grunting fools, thick cunts,
with their annoying husbands. Glad I don't have to put up
with any of them men. Pricks.
                    clench
          release
      breathe deep
Check my phone   04.47.   I lean my head on the window
and look out where cars spin round the roundabout
turning out and in of the supermarket car-park.
Signs shout   OPEN 24/7   EVERY LITTLE HELPS
Rain drizzles down, fizzes into puddles.
                    clench
          release
      breathe deep
Something wants to break free of me. Someone. Stranger.
Traffic lights reflect colour on wet road, all red orange green
red orange green, red orange green.
I watch the colours and do my breathing like they showed me:
                    clench
          release
      breathe deep
red orange green, red orange green … Then this stupid
      fucking Subaru
roars up, pimply boy racer revving, bass thrumming, elbow out
his window, flash of a lighter, curl of smoke winding up in the air.
He turns his head and stares at me, all the way up here.

Cheeky bastard.

                  clench

            release

      breathe deep

and he's still there, still staring. I give him the finger, mouth
WANKER
Surely he can't see me … can he? I'm just one of a hundred fools
in flowery nighties in a hundred hospital windows…

                  clench

            release

      breathe deep

I look away. Back. He's still there. Still, he stares.
The lights still red red red. Road shines in rain.

                  clench

            release

      breathe deep

Can he see me? I don't know. Then suddenly, it all changes in me,
hardens. I make stiff fists, hold the windowsill.

                  CLENCH

            release

      breathe deep

When I look up, he's gone. The night is over, the streetlights off.
The traffic lights have changed.
Green.
Go.

Notes

The Horse Under The Hearth, p. 12
"Though [*Caoineadh Airt Uí Laoghaire* by Eibhlín Dubh Ní Chonaill] castigates Eibhlín's brother-in-law Baldwin ... for handing the horse over to his great enemy after Art's death, it's known that she had the animal stolen back. The horse was later shot and had its head buried under the flagstone in the parlour of Rath Laoi House."—*Cork Literary Review*, Volume 13, 2009, p. 162.

Valise of Memories, p. 14
Margaret Maher was an Irish maid who worked for Emily Dickinson. They shared a deep bond, and Dickinson stored her poems in Maher's trunk. Despite her vow to burn the poems after her mistress's death, Maher passed them on to Dickinson's family. For more, see Aífe Murray's *Maid as Muse* (University Press of New England, 2010).

Frozen Food, p. 22
During scientific analysis of the Hauslabjoch mummy, it was revealed that he had been carrying a sloe berry.

Bone Flute, p. 29
In 2009, archaeologists discovered the oldest known musical instrument — a 35,000 year old flute made from the wing bone of a mute swan.

Inventory: Recovery Room, p. 35
beestings: sometimes known as green or yellow milk; the nutrient-rich colostrum of a cow.

Electrocardiogram, p. 52

The ECG is a machine that measures cardiac activity. The etymology of the word derives from Greek — *electro* (the heart's electrical activity), *cardio* (the heart) and *graph* (to write) — this machine writes the story of the heart.

Tapetum Lucidum p. 57

(Latin: "bright tapestry') A layer of tissue in the eye of many vertebrates that reflects light, contributing to night vision. *Lamping*: hunting using a torch; many nocturnal animals will stand very still when a torch is shone directly at them.

At Letterfrack, p. 62

St Joseph's Industrial School was an institution for boys run by the Christian Brothers in Letterfrack, Galway from 1887 to its closure in 1974. While in the care of the school, 147 children died. Accounts of the horrific abuse and neglect endured by these children is detailed in the *Report of the Commission to Inquire into Child Abuse* (2009).